Mottos
to Live By

Blue Mountain Press®

Boulder, Colorado

Mottos
to Live By

A collection of poems
Edited by Susan Polis Schutz

Blue Mountain Press ®

Boulder, Colorado

Copyright © 1993 by Stephen Schutz and Susan Polis Schutz.
Copyright © 1993 by Blue Mountain Arts, Inc.

Library of Congress Catalog Card Number: 93-30909
ISBN: 0-88396-370-1

ACKNOWLEDGMENTS appear on page 64.

design on book cover is registered in
U.S. Patent and Trademark Office.

Manufactured in the United States of America
First Printing: August, 1993

Library of Congress Cataloging-in-Publication Data

Mottos to live by : a collection of poems / edited by Susan Polis
    Schutz.
        p.   cm.
    ISBN 0-88396-370-1
    1. Didactic poetry, American.   2. Conduct of life—Poetry.
I. Schutz, Susan Polis.
PS309.D53M68   1993
811.008 '0353—dc20

                                                    93-30909
                                                        CIP

This book is printed on fine quality, laid embossed, 80 lb. paper. This paper has been
specially produced to be acid free (neutral pH) and contains no groundwood or
unbleached pulp. It conforms with all of the requirements of the American National
Standards Institute, Inc., so as to ensure that this book will last and be enjoyed by
future generations.

Blue Mountain Press ®

P.O. Box 4549, Boulder, Colorado 80306

CONTENTS

A Motto to Live By

When the world gets you down,
put things in perspective.
Move ahead in a positive way;
    don't allow yourself to become mired
        in a negative view.
See things for what they really are.
Don't let the little things get in the way.
Do what you can, however you can,
    with the resources you have available
        to you.
Don't sell yourself short;
    you have the power within you
        to change what needs changing.
Face the situation with the resolve
    to remedy it; do what you need to do
        to put it behind you.
Move ahead in the direction of happiness;
    go for your dreams
        and reach for your star.

And remember who's in
    the driver's seat: you are.

—Collin McCarty

Always Listen
to Your Own Heart

You cannot listen
to what others
want you to do
You must listen
to yourself
Society
family
friends
and loved ones
do not know what
you must do
Only you know
and only you
can do what is
right for you

So start right now
You will need to
work very hard
You will need to
overcome many obstacles
You will need to go
against the better
judgment of some people
and you will need to
bypass their prejudices
But you can have
whatever you want
if you try hard enough

So start right now and
you will live
a life designed
by you and
for you
and you will
love
your
life

—Susan Polis Schutz

You Can Do
Anything You Set Your Mind To

There is no task,
large or small,
that can't be completed
if you set your mind
to it.
Always remember
that you are as strong
as you
allow yourself to be.

When someone says "defeat,"
think success —
when someone says "lose,"
think win —
when someone says "can't,"
think that you can —
and if anyone ever tells you
that you "won't,"
tell them that you
most certainly will.

—Beth Fagan Quinn

Keep Believing in Yourself

There may be days
when you get up in the morning
and things aren't the way
you had hoped they would be.
That's when you have to
tell yourself that things will get better.
There are times when people
disappoint you and let you down,
but those are the times
when you must remind yourself
to trust your own judgments and opinions,
to keep your life focused on believing in yourself
and all that you are capable of.
There will be challenges to face
and changes to make in your life,
and it is up to you to accept them.

Constantly keep yourself headed
in the right direction for you.
It may not be easy at times,
but in those times of struggle
you will find a stronger sense of who you are,
and you will also see yourself
developing into the person
you have always wanted to be.

Life is a journey through time,
filled with many choices;
each of us will experience life
in our own special way.
So when the days come that are filled
with frustration and unexpected responsibilities,
remember to believe in yourself
and all you want your life to be,
because the challenges and changes
will only help you to find the dreams
that you know are meant to come true for you.

—Deanna Beisser

There Is Greatness Within You

Throughout your life, always pursue
sensitivity and kindness
   as your chosen way.
A sense of humor is wonderful;
   hold on to yours.
Being able to laugh at the world
   will see you through many hard times.
Guard against bitterness and sarcasm;
   they can destroy you.
Be yourself; the world will benefit
   from your talent.
Search for people who love and
   appreciate you for who you are
and who encourage you to improve.
Don't be satisfied with less
   than all you can be,
for you have greatness within you.

—Bill Cross

A List of the "Don'ts and Do's" That Will Always See You Through

Don't ever stop dreaming your dreams;
    they're a very essential part of you.
Do whatever you can to make them a
    reality by the course you take,
        the plans you make,
            and all the things you do.
Don't dwell on past mistakes; leave
    yesterday behind you — along with any
    of its problems, worries, and doubts.
Do realize you can't change the past,
    but just ahead is the future — and
    you _can_ do something about that.

Don't try to accomplish everything at
   once; life can be difficult enough —
   without adding frustration to the list.
Do travel one step at a time, and reach
   for one goal at a time. That's the way
   to find out what real accomplishment is.
Don't be afraid to do the impossible,
   even if others don't think you'll succeed.
Do remember that history is filled with
   incredible accomplishments of those who
      were foolish enough . . . to believe.
Don't forget that there are so many
   things that are wonderful, rare,
      and unique about you.
And do remember that if you can search
   within and find a smile . . . that smile
      will always be a reflection
      of the way people feel . . . about you.

                              —Collin McCarty

This Life Is Yours

This life is yours
Believe in yourself
Take the power
to choose what you want to do
and do it well
Take the power
to love what you want in life
and love it honestly
Take the power
to walk in the forest
and be a part of nature
Take the power
to control your own life
No one else can do it for you
Nothing is too good for you
You deserve the best
Take the power
to make your life
healthy
exciting
worthwhile
and very happy
Take the power
to create your own dreams
and make them come true

—Susan Polis Schutz

Live Each Day with Love

Life is a constant process
   of growth and change.
Each day is a miracle filled
with new discoveries
and challenges.
Some days bring hurt
   and disappointment also,
but these, too, are challenges,
and as you grow and change
you learn to handle them
   with more ease.

Growing older means growing
in experience,
growing in courage and
   compassion,
growing in love,
and growing in strength.
Growing older means changing
your life to make it meaningful
   to you,
changing your attitudes,
and staying flexible about
everyday living.

Life keeps getting better
as long as you have
a positive attitude.

Remind yourself
   of all the things
you love about life,
stay in touch with your
   loved ones and friends,
and do what your own heart
tells you to.
Your tomorrow will always bring
you good things if you
live each day with love.

—Donna Levine

18 Ways to Make
Each Day of Your Life
Happier

Every day . . .
Share a kind word with a friend.
Give away a smile.
Tell one secret.
Listen to what someone has to say.
Listen with your heart
   to what someone cannot say.
Try one new thing.
Forgive one person who has hurt you.
Forgive yourself for past mistakes.
Realize your imperfections.
Discover your possibilities.
Make a new friend.
Accept responsibility
   for everything you do.
Refuse responsibility
   for anyone else's actions.
Dream one dream.
Watch the sunset.
Cherish what you have.
Cherish who you are.
Love your life.

—Vickie M. Worsham

"For This One Day"

I want you to begin this day anew, with the thought of becoming the person you'd like to be. Today I want you to set aside some time just for you . . . to plan, to dream, to be honest with yourself about yourself. May you become better acquainted with the wonderful person you are.

Today I want you to experience something new. I want you to learn from the world around you: from the words you read, the sounds you hear, the touches you feel, and the faces you see. Even through the course of your daily tasks, may you try to search for a new perspective, lean towards understanding, and make the commonplace a wondrous place to be. Make your happiness . . . a happiness that lasts.

I want you to think of your friends and loved ones — and be warmed by knowing that they hold on to some very meaningful thoughts of you. May you have a gentle thanks for the sunrises and smiles, along with the hardships and trials, that have helped to make you what you are today.

I wish you the kind of intuition that lets you know how naturally joy comes to those who open their eyes wide enough to envision it. I wish you the realization that — by some interesting twist — doing for others is also doing for you.

I wish you the luxury of being reminded that having a sense of humor helps you to survive, and that even when everything else goes wrong, it pays such nice dividends to simply be glad you're a part of this moment in time. I wish you the simple pleasure of being alive.

May you listen to your inner needs and comply as best as you can. For today, I wish you a little learning for your mind, as much love as your heart can hold, nourishment and exercise for your body, and being able to see the beauty of the world . . . for your soul.

Today I want you to think of the past only long enough to learn from it. And I hope you'll glance ahead to the future only for a fleeting dream you hope will come true. Today is your day. Your moment in time. Make it work . . . for you.

—Collin McCarty

How you live today
affects all of your tomorrows.
Remember that turning down
the wrong road
is part of the journey,
and finding the way back
is your challenge.
Remember that if you keep love
close to your heart,
home will never be far away.
There will be expectations not met,
promises lost, tears,
and moments of despair.
Remember, however,
to be grateful for the sunshine
and to find hope in the rainbow.
Remember to laugh from your soul
and always hold on to your dreams.

—Bernadette Garzarelli

A Creed for All of Us

The world was made
to be beautiful —
but sometimes we get caught up in
everyday actions
completely forgetting about this
completely forgetting that
what is truly important
are the simple, basic things in life —
honest, pure emotions
surrounded by the majestic beauty
    of nature
We need to concentrate on
the freeness and peacefulness of nature
and not on the driven material aspects
    of life
We need to smell the clear air
after the rainfall
and appreciate the good in things

Each of us must be responsible
	and do our part
in order to help preserve a
	beautiful world —
the waterfalls, the oceans, the mountains
the large gray boulders
the large green farms
the fluffy pink clouds
the sunrise and sunsets, ladybugs
rainbows, dew, hummingbirds
butterflies, dandelions
We need to remember that
we are here for a short time
and that every day
	should count for something
and that every day
	we should be thankful
for all the natural beauty
The world is a wonderful place
and we are so lucky to be a part of it

—Susan Polis Schutz

You Can Make a
Difference in Your World

It's not how much you accomplish in life
that really counts,
but how much you give to others.
It's not how high you build your dreams
that makes a difference,
but how high your faith can climb.
It's not how many goals you reach,
but how many lives you touch.
It's not who you know that matters,
but who you are inside.

Believe in the impossible,
hold tight to the incredible,
and live each day to its fullest potential.
You can make a difference in your world.

—Rebecca Barlow Jordan

Be Proud of Who You Are

Pride is loving yourself for who you are
and who you will become;
it's a gentle knowledge of
your strengths and weaknesses,
a respect for yourself because
you are a unique human being.
Pride is loving the things you do
and doing whatever it takes to do them well;
it's being concerned with the little details
and taking the time to work on them.
Pride is knowing that you have the courage
to withstand the pressures
and disappointments of life;
it's having dignity when faced
with difficult situations,
and maintaining your self-esteem
even when things are not going well.

Pride is having the ability to laugh at yourself,
to know that your mistakes
are only steppingstones to your success.
Pride is loving the world around you
and being glad to offer help
to someone who needs a friend;
it's speaking and thinking
of all the good you see,
giving encouragement where you can,
and listening to those around you.
Pride is feeling good about yourself
and doing the things that make you happy.
It's being interested and enthusiastic about life;
it's giving yourself to life
as well as accepting the best that life has for you.

—Donna Levine

Don't Ever Be
Afraid to Be Yourself

In a world of comparisons
and conformity,
make your own statement.
Honor your own truth.
Have the courage to be yourself;
risk speaking your own thoughts
and claiming your emotions.
Share your vulnerabilities,
fears, doubts, and insecurities;
let others experience the real you.
Have the courage to be yourself,
and realize that you are
a wonderful person.

—Diane Holcomb

Life Is as Beautiful
as You Make It

Always live your life to its fullest.
Enjoy laughter, touch a star.
Smile for today
while you shine through your tomorrows.
Open your heart to strangers;
destiny may bring newfound friends.
Venture out, conquer the unconquerable.
Look where others dare not look,
and question all that is questionable.
Remember that happiness is the home
we build within ourselves.
Speak your mind.
Hear a symphony within silence.
Open your heart.
Challenge tomorrows
and treasure yesterdays.
Capture all that you can
in this beautiful creation called life.

—William J. Burrows

Promise Yourself

Promise yourself to be so strong that nothing can disturb your peace of mind. To talk health, happiness and prosperity to every person you meet. To make all your friends feel that there is something in them. To look at the sunny side of everything and make your optimism come true. To think only of the best, to work only for the best and expect only the best. To be just as enthusiastic about the success of others as you are about your own. To forget the mistakes of the past and press on to the greater achievements of the future. To wear a cheerful countenance at all times and give every living creature you meet a smile. To give so much time to the improvement of yourself that you have no time to criticize others. To be too large for worry, too noble for anger, too strong for fear and too happy to permit the presence of trouble.

—Christian D. Larson

No Matter
What Dark Clouds
May Come Your Way,
Keep on Shining
like the Sun

We all know that
no matter how many clouds
get in the way,
the sun keeps on shining.
No matter how many times its rays
are blocked from our view,
the sun will reappear on another day
to shine more brilliantly than before.
It takes determination
to outlast those dark clouds
that sometimes enter your life,
and patience to keep on shining
no matter what gets in your way.
But it all pays off eventually.
One of these days
when you least expect it,
you'll overcome your difficulties,
because you and the sun
have a lot in common:
You're both going to shine
no matter what.

—Barbara J. Hall

Patience

Patience is learning how to wait
when you really don't want to.
It's discovering things you like to do
while you're waiting,
and becoming so happy with
what you're doing that you
forget you're waiting.
Patience is taking time every day
to dream your dreams
and develop the confidence in yourself
to change your dreams into reality.
Patience is being good to yourself
and having the faith to hold on to your dreams,
even as days go by when you can't see
how they will come true.
Patience is loving others
even when they disappoint you
and you don't understand them.
It's knowing how to let go
and accept others as they are
and forgive them for things they have done.

Patience is loving yourself
and giving yourself time to grow;
it's doing things that keep you
healthy and happy,
and it's knowing that you deserve
the best in life
and are willing to work for it,
no matter how long it takes.
Patience is being willing to face
whatever challenges life gives you,
realizing that life has also given you
the strength and courage to endure
and deal with each challenge.
Patience is the ability to
continue to love and laugh
no matter what your circumstances may be,
because you recognize that in time
those circumstances will change,
and that love and laughter
are what give life deeper meaning,
and you the determination
to continue to have patience.

—Donna Levine

Life Isn't Always Easy

Life can be unfair at times,
and those are the times
when you must maintain faith
and never let go.
It is especially during the difficult times
that you must live your life
to its fullest potential.
Those are the times to triumph
over circumstances
with hope and courage.
Life isn't always easy,
but if you keep going and persevere
to the very best of your ability,
you will gain strength to manage
the new challenges ahead.
Each goal that you reach
is another important step forward.
Believe that there are
bright and wonderful days
ahead for you,
and you will find them.

—Mary A. Rothman

Courage

Courage is the strength
to stand up when it's
easier to fall down.
It is the conviction
to explore new horizons
when it's easier
to believe what we've been told.

Courage is the desire to maintain
our integrity when it's easier
to look the other way.
It is feeling happy and alive
when it's easier to feel
sorry for ourselves.

Courage is the will to shape
our world when it's easier
to let someone else do it for us.
It is the recognition
that none of us are perfect,
when it's easier to criticize others.

Courage is the power to step forward
and lead when it's easier
to follow the crowd.
It is the spirit that places you
on top of the mountain
when it's easier
to never leave the ground.

Courage is the freedom
of our mind, body, and soul.

—John Carzello

Hold On Tightly to What Is Truly Important in Life

Hold on to faith; it is the source of believing that all things are possible. It is the fiber and strength of a confident soul.

Hold on to hope; it banishes doubt and enables attitudes to be positive and cheerful.

Hold on to trust; it is at the core of fruitful relationships that are secure and content.

Hold on to love; it is life's greatest gift of all, for it shares, cares, and gives meaning to life.

Hold on to family and friends; they are the most important people in your life, and they make the world a better place. They are your roots and the beginnings that you grew from; they are the vine that has grown through time to nourish you, help you on your way, and always remain close by.

Hold on to all that you are and all that you have learned, for these things are what make you unique. Don't ignore what you feel and what you believe is right and important; your heart has a way of speaking louder than your mind.

Hold on to your dreams; achieve them diligently and honestly. Never take the easy way or surrender to deceit. Remember others on your way, and take time to care for their needs. Enjoy the beauty around you. Have the courage to see things differently and clearly. Make the world a better place one day at a time, and don't let go of the important things that give meaning to your life.

—Kelly D. Caron

Hope is not pretending
that troubles don't exist.
It is the trust
that they will not last forever,
that hurts will be healed
   and difficulties overcome.
It is faith that
a source of strength and renewal
   lies within
to lead us through the dark
   into the sunshine.

—Elizabeth A. Chase

The True Secret of Happiness

Every day, have
something to do
or somewhere to go
Every day have
someone to call
someone to see
someone to love
But most important
every day have
something to give
to someone

—Natasha Josefowitz

Be Thankful for All
the Gifts You've Been Given

Believe that you have the innate ability
to become all you are capable of becoming.

Forget the problems that don't matter anymore,
the tears that cried themselves away,
and the worries that will wash away
   on the shore of tomorrow.

Determine your own worth
by yourself,
and do not be dependent
on another's judgment of you.

Teach love
   to those who know hate.

Dare to dream,
and live those dreams,
for it is in your dreams
that you can begin to realize
your true destiny.
Live with an aliveness,
a joy, a wonder
for all the gifts
you've been given.

—Debbi Oehman

All the Great Things
Improve with Time

Like wisdom handed down
   through the years.
And the trees as they so
   wonderfully grow.
Like wine as it gently ages.
And rivers as they flow.

Like memories that keep getting better.
And the bond between friends.
Like happiness and serenity.
And love that never ends.

All the great things improve with time.
With qualities that become more dear.
Like people who were incredibly special
   to begin with.
And who keep getting better each year.

—Casey Whilson

You Can Accomplish
Anything You Choose

Try to see yourself as you really are —
powerful, sensitive, determined,
   and gracious.
See yourself achieving everything
   you choose to achieve
and being exactly
who and what you want to be.

See yourself flourishing
and conquering all limitations.
See yourself for who you really are
and what you are capable of —
someone who can accomplish anything.

—Lea Marie Tomlyn

Always Do Your Best

Find your strength. Search for that smile of yours that makes everything brighter. Hang in there, even though that can be easier said than done. Have faith.

Don't give up. Make a commitment . . . between your determination, your hopes, and your heart . . . that your sun _is_ going to shine in the sky. Live your life a day at a time, and things will get better by and by.

Find your way through the days with the light that shines within you. Leave a smile where there wasn't one before. Help a hurt; make it mend. Find the strength to make things right again.

Go forward, from one steppingstone to another. Reach out a little farther. If you believe you can, then you _will_ make it through. Listen a little more often to what your heart has to say. Do the things that are important to you.

Make today everything you dreamed it could be. Don't settle for less. Use the precious hours you've been given as wisely as you can. Always do your best.

—Chris Gallatin

Find Happiness
in Everything You Do

People will get only what they seek
Choose your goals carefully
Know what you like
and what you do not like
Be critical about what you can do well
and what you cannot do well
Choose a career or lifestyle that interests you
and work hard to make it a success
but also have fun in what you do
Be honest with people
    and help them if you can
but don't depend on anyone
    to make life easy or happy for you
(only you can do that for yourself)
Be strong and decisive
but remain sensitive
Regard your family, and the idea of a family
as the basis for security, support and love

Understand who you are
and what you want in life
before sharing your life with someone
When you are ready to enter a relationship
make sure that the person is worthy of
everything you are physically and mentally

Strive to achieve all that you want
Find happiness in everything you do
Love with your entire being
Love with an uninhibited soul
Make a triumph
of every aspect
of your life

—Susan Polis Schutz

Within You Is the Strength
to Meet Life's Challenges

You are stronger than you think —
  remember to stand tall.
Every challenge in your life
  helps you to grow.
Every problem you encounter
  strengthens your mind and your soul.
Every trouble you overcome
  increases your understanding of life.
When all your troubles weigh heavily
  on your shoulders,
remember that beneath the burden
  you can stand tall,
because you are never given
  more than you can handle —
and you are stronger
  than you think.

—Lisa Wroble

Remember These Words...

Don't let go of hope.
Hope gives you the strength to keep going
when you feel like giving up.
Don't ever quit believing in yourself.
As long as you believe you can,
you will have a reason for trying.
Don't let anyone hold
your happiness in their hands;
hold it in yours,
so it will always be within your reach.
Don't measure success or failure
by material wealth, but by how you feel;
our feelings determine the richness of our lives.
Don't let bad moments overcome you;
be patient, and they will pass.
Don't hesitate to reach out for help;
we all need it from time to time.
Don't run away from love but towards love,
because it is our deepest joy.

Don't wait for what you want to come to you;
go after it with all that you are,
knowing that life will meet you halfway.
Don't feel like you've lost
when plans and dreams fall short of your hopes.
Anytime you learn something new
about yourself or about life,
you have progressed.
Don't do anything that takes away
from your self-respect;
feeling good about yourself
is essential to feeling good about life.
Don't ever forget how to laugh
or be too proud to cry.
It is by doing both that we live life to its fullest.

—Nancye Sims

Take Each Day
One at a Time

One day
at a time —
this is enough.
Do not look back
and grieve over
   the past,
for it is gone,
and do not be troubled
about the future,
for it has not yet come.
Live in the present,
and make it so beautiful
that it will be worth
   remembering.

—Ida Scott Taylor

ACKNOWLEDGMENTS

The following is a partial list of authors whom the publisher especially wishes to thank for permission to reprint their works.

Beth Fagan Quinn for "You Can Do Anything. . . ." Copyright © 1993 by Beth Fagan Quinn. All rights reserved. Reprinted by permission.

Vickie M. Worsham for "18 Ways to Make Each Day. . . ." Copyright © 1993 by Vickie M. Worsham. All rights reserved. Reprinted by permission.

Donna Levine for "Be Proud of Who You Are," and "Patience." Copyright © 1993 by Donna Levine. All rights reserved. Reprinted by permission.

Diane Holcomb for "Don't Ever Be Afraid. . . ." Copyright © 1993 by Diane Holcomb. All rights reserved. Reprinted by permission.

William J. Burrows for "Life Is as Beautiful. . . ." Copyright © 1993 by William J. Burrows. All rights reserved. Reprinted by permission.

John Carzello for "Courage." Copyright © 1993 by John Carzello. All rights reserved. Reprinted by permission.

Kelly D. Caron for "Hold On Tightly. . . ." Copyright © 1993 by Kelly D. Caron. All rights reserved. Reprinted by permission.

Elizabeth A. Chase for "Hope is not pretending. . . ." Copyright © 1993 by Elizabeth A. Chase. All rights reserved. Reprinted by permission.

Natasha Josefowitz for "The True Secret of Happiness." Copyright © 1991 by Natasha Josefowitz. All rights reserved. Reprinted by permission.

A careful effort has been made to trace the ownership of poems used in this anthology in order to obtain permission to reprint copyrighted materials and to give proper credit to the copyright owners. If any error or omission has occurred, it is completely inadvertent, and we would like to make corrections in future editions provided that written notification is made to the publisher:

BLUE MOUNTAIN PRESS, INC., P.O. Box 4549, Boulder, Colorado 80306.